WHAT'S WRONG AT THE WINTER CARNIVAL?

ILLUSTRATED BY JOHN HOLLADAY

There are five things wrong
in each colorful scene.
Can you find them all?

SMITHMARK

THE GONDOLA

HOLIDAY TIME

WARMING UP

SNOWBALL FIGHT

ANSWERS

There are five things wrong in each scene.

THE GONDOLA (1) surfer; (2) man skiing on pencils; (3) golf clubs instead of skis on gondola; (4) upside-down tree; (5) skier on roof of house.

HOLIDAY TIME (1) tree with green leaves; (2) triangular window frame instead of half circle; (3) horse wearing boot; (4) fish in window of house; (5) square wheel on stagecoach.

ICEBOATING (1) pizza slice instead of sail; (2) scuba diver in boat; (3) baseball player in crowd; (4) pail of daisies; (5) sailboat in background instead of iceboat.

ICE-SKATING (1) giant ice-cream cone between trees; (2) boy wearing graduation cap; (3) candy cane instead of lamppost; (4) tulips in flower box; (5) ducks swimming on ice.